Ricl

The Inspirational Story of Football Superstar Richard Sherman

Copyright 2015 by Bill Redban - All rights reserved.

This document is geared towards providing exact and reliable information in regards to the topic and issue covered. The publication is sold with the idea that the publisher is not required to render accounting, officially permitted, or otherwise, qualified services. If advice is necessary, legal or professional, a practiced individual in the profession should be ordered.

In no way is it legal to reproduce, duplicate, or transmit any part of this document in either electronic means or in printed format. Recording of this publication is strictly prohibited and any storage of this document is not allowed unless with written permission from the publisher. All rights reserved.

The information provided herein is stated to be truthful and consistent, in that any liability, in terms of inattention or otherwise, by any usage or abuse of any policies, processes, or directions contained within is the solitary and utter responsibility of the recipient reader. Under no circumstances will any legal responsibility or blame be held against the publisher for any reparation, damages, or monetary loss due to the information herein, either directly or indirectly.

The information herein is offered for informational purposes solely, and is universal as so. The presentation of the information is without contract or any type of guarantee assurance.

The trademarks that are used are without any consent, and the publication of the trademark is without permission or backing by the trademark owner. All trademarks and brands within this book are for clarifying purposes only and are the owned by the owners themselves, not affiliated with this document.

Table Of Contents

Introduction

Chapter 1: Youth & Family Life

Chapter 2: College

Chapter 3: Professional Life

Chapter 4: Personal Adult Life

Chapter 5: Philanthropic/Charitable Acts

Chapter 6: Legacy, Potential & Inspiration

Chapter 7: Notable Statistics & Career Milestones

Conclusion

Introduction

As the title already implies, this is a book about [The Inspirational Story of Football Superstar Richard Sherman] and how he rose from his life in Compton, California to becoming one of today's leading and most-respected football players. In his rise to superstardom, Richard has inspired not only the youth, but fans of all ages throughout the world.

This book also portrays the struggles that Richard has had to overcome during his early childhood years, his teen years, and up until he became what he is today. A notable source of inspiration is Richard's own foundation, as well as his consistent support of other charitable organizations. He continues to serve as the polarizing, fan-friendly superstar in a sport that glorifies flashy plays and mega personalities.

Combining impressive size, overwhelming athleticism, elite instincts, and superior coordination, Richard has shown the ability to impact a game in a variety of ways. From being a young athlete who could play multiple sports to becoming perhaps the most suffocating defensive player of his generation, you'll learn here how this man has risen to the ranks of the best football players today.

Thanks again for downloading this book. I hope you are able to take some lessons from Richard's life and apply them to your own!

Chapter 1:

Youth & Family Life

Richard Sherman was welcomed to the world on March 30th, 1988. He was born to father, Kevin, and mother, Beverley, in Compton, California. Richard also grew up with an older brother named Branton. His father was, and still is, a committed garbage collector for over thirty years. His work ethic and commitment were character traits that would be instilled in young Richard. Richard saw his father wake up at 4am each morning to go to work, with no excuses.

Because of Kevin's experience in gang culture, he was able to show Richard and Branton the negative effects first hand. Not only was he involved in criminal activity as a youngster, but he survived two gun shots and still has the wounds to prove it. This wisdom would serve his two sons well, as Richard internalized what could happen to him if he did not keep his head on straight.

Richard was able to stay out of gang life and instead put his focus towards his school work and sports. Showing a natural inclination to athletics, Richard harnessed his physical gifts and began to take interest in playing the sport of football. Branton was a few years older than Richard and served as a source of motivation. Brandon was an athlete in his own right, running track throughout high school.

Upon entering the ninth grade, Richard chose to enroll at Dominguez High School. He showed immediate potential as an athlete and became involved with football and track and field. In track and field, Richard excelled at the triple jump. He was able to win the California state title in the event, with a total mark of 15.44 meters. Furthermore, Richard also made it to the state finals in the 110-meter hurdles, where he finished third with a time of 13.99 seconds. He finished sixth in the long jump and recorded a 10.77 second run in the 110 meters. Richard was so good that he was given All-American honors for his accomplishments in the triple jump.

On the football field, Richard's tall lanky build worked to his advantage. He played wide receiver, defensive back, and punt returner during his time with Dominguez High School. His senior year was truly spectacular, as he totaled over 1,000 all-purpose yards for the season, including 28 catches and three punt return touchdowns. Defensively, Richard recorded almost fifty tackles, broke up eight passes, and recorded one interception. More importantly, the team would have success on the field - a theme that we will continue to see in Richard's career. Dominguez went on to win the CIF Southern Section state championship game with a victory over Sherman Oaks High School by a score of 41-14.

Despite all of his on-field success, Richard took care of business in the class room as well. He graduated from Dominguez High School as the salutatorian (ranked second) of his class. With a graduating GPA of over 4.0, Richard was the definition of a strong student-athlete. One instance that is representative of Richard's dedication to his schoolwork, was when he made USC head football coach Pete Carroll wait for two and a half hours to discuss his interest to play for the school - all because he didn't want to leave class early.

As you would expect, a player of Richard's pedigree received quite a bit of courting from college programs. However, in the end, Richard and his family decided that Stanford University would be the best fit to match Richard's values. Richard's academic inclination also contributed to his decision, as a degree from Stanford University is considered to be one of the most prestigious in the world.

Chapter 2:

College

Richard's athletic scholarship to Stanford University covered all four years and it would serve as the next chapter in his life. Now living in the affluent area of Palo Alto, California, Richard would embark on his journey as a student-athlete for the Stanford Cardinal. He became a member of Phi Beta Sigma fraternity and soon became one of the most recognizable students on campus.

He began his freshman year as a wide receiver for the team and went on to lead the team in receiving yards by the end of the season. His accomplishments would be recognized on the national level, as he was named a Freshman All-American. He continued his solid play as the team's go-to wide receiver in his second season until he suffered an unfortunate injury early in the 2008 season.

His season-ending knee injury forced him to miss the remainder of the 2008-09 season and Richard used the off-season to rehabilitate his knee while also building his body up even further. Upon returning to the team, Richard was converted from a wide receiver to a cornerback. This change was made due to the combination of the team desperately needing a reliable corner, as well as Richard's own abilities to play the position.

Over his final two years at Stanford, Richard totaled 112 tackles to go along with six interceptions. Furthermore, he was able to lock down the opposing team's best receiver on multiple occasions. In 2010, Richard's last season with the team, the Stanford Cardinal was able to finish the year with a 12-1 record. With Richard's impact on the defensive side of the ball, along with Andrew Luck running the offense, Stanford was ranked as one of the best teams in the entire country.

Richard went on to graduate after the 2010 season with a Bachelor's degree in Communications. By the time he played his last game with the team, Richard was already working on his Master's degree. His well-rounded character as a superb student-athlete was shown once again and Richard was recognized nationally for this accomplishment.

Richard was also able to continue competing in track and field during his time at Stanford. He participated in the triple jump and 110 meter hurdles and was a nationally-ranked athlete in these at the collegiate level. If Richard had not pursued professional football, he certainly could have had a career as a track and field athlete.

Chapter 3:

Professional Life

First Season

On draft day, it was not clear where Richard would go or in what round he would be selected in. Despite a decorated high school and college career, Richard was not perceived as one of the best cornerback prospects in the draft. Although his knee injury was two years behind him, some teams did not want to take a risk on him because they feared he could be injury prone. Others were not convinced that he could keep up with receivers at the NFL level.

Nevertheless, the Seattle Seahawks believed in Richard's potential and chose him in the fifth round of the 2011 NFL Draft. Richard was not pleased with the amount of players that he perceived as inferior being drafted before him, and he entered the National Football League with a huge chip on his shoulder.

With no real outside expectations heading into his rookie season, Richard focused on working hard and performing as well as he could on Sundays. He started ten games in his first season and by season's end, Richard was a full-time starter for the team. He played so well that he was chosen as a member of the 2011 Pro Football Weekly All-Rookie Team. His statistics for his first year consisted of seventeen passes defensed, four interceptions, and a total of 55 tackles. This combination of statistics for a player who did not enter the season as the designated starter, signaled that Richard had potential to become one of the best young corners in the game.

Second Season

Richard entered his second season under Coach Pete Carroll as the starting cornerback for the team. Many football experts around the league were predicting the Seahawks to make a big jump from the previous year, mainly because of the loaded talent that they had accumulated on their roster. Richard, along with his teammates on defense, were looking to turn the Seahawks into a defensive force to be reckoned with.

Just before Seattle's Week 8 match-up against the Detroit Lions, Richard nicknamed himself "Optimus Prime", a statement showing that he intended to lock down Detroit's Calvin Johnson, who's nickname is "Megatron". While Calvin did not get completely shut down, Richard and the Seattle defense held him to just three catches and under fifty yards for the game - much below his averages for the season.

In Week 14 when the Seahawks faced the Arizona Cardinals, Richard picked off Cardinals' quarterback John Skelton twice, returning one of them for a touchdown. Additionally, Richard recorded two tackles, an assisted tackle, as well as a fumble recovery. His efforts were key in Seattle's demolition of Arizona, resulting in a 58-0 shutout - the biggest shutout in Seahawks franchise history.

Week 16 served as another big game in Richard's breakout season, when the Seahawks played division rival, San Francisco. Richard recorded five tackles and an interception, while also making his presence felt on special teams. He recovered a blocked field goal and returned it ninety yards for a touchdown.

Heading into Week 17 of his second season, Richard had already recorded 61 tackles, three forced fumbles, and seven interceptions on the season. It was painfully obvious that he was one of the best cornerbacks in the entire league and he had the statistics to prove it. However, Richard surprisingly did not make the 2012 Pro Bowl. Most experts around the league agreed that Richard was one of the biggest snubs for the team. However, by season's end, Richard was selected to the Associated Press All-Pro First Team, an honor that is even harder to earn than a Pro Bowl selection.

The Seahawks had a much improved season in Richard's second year and were able to make the NFC Playoffs. While the San Francisco 49ers won the AFC West division title, the Seahawks earned a berth by taking one of the two Wild Card slots. The team's first round match-up against the Washington Redskins resulted in a victory. After moving on to face the top-ranked Atlanta Falcons, the Seahawks suffered a two-point loss in a valiant effort on the road.

Despite the heart-breaking end to the season, the Seattle players and fans had much to be proud of. The team showed that it could compete with some of the best teams in the league and it was obvious that they had a great deal of potential heading into the next season.

Third Season

Richard's third pre-season started off much differently than the previous two. Not only was he publicly accepted as one of the best defensive backs in football, but the team entered the year with high expectations. Many around the league considered Seattle one of the favorites to win the Super Bowl, along with the Denver Broncos, and division-rival San Francisco 49ers.

Richard, along with the other members of the Seahawks defensive backfield, began calling themselves the "Legion of Boom" because of their hard hitting style and their ability to lock up receivers one on one. The Legion of Boom lived up to expectations, as they went on to allow the fewest passing yards in the entire National Football League. The Seattle defense was the best in the league and their defensive backs were a large reason why.

Richard would continue his personal improvement, as he led the league with eight interceptions for the season. He was finally named to his first Pro Bowl and was the top vote-getter among all defensive players. Furthermore, he was named to the Associated Press All-Pro First Team for the second consecutive year.

As a team, the Seahawks would have a year to remember. They played a dominant regular season on both offense and defense and really honed in on developing their identity as a defense and run oriented team. They earned the number one seed in the NFC standings and entered the Playoffs on a high note. After a first-round bye, Seattle went on to face the New Orleans Saints at home. By this time, it was well-known that the Seattle Seahawks had one of the biggest home-field advantages in the entire NFL. Seattle was able to win the game by a score of 23-15, and the Legion of Boom held a Drew Brees-led offense to under 20 points - quite an impressive feat.

The win set up an NFC Championship game match-up between the Seahawks and San Francisco 49ers. The game was played in Seattle and was one of the most-anticipated games of the season. Richard was integral in the Seattle victory, as on the last play, he was targeted by 49ers' quarterback Colin Kaepernick in the back of the end zone. Richard made a game-saving play when he batted the ball away, resulting in a Seahawks interception.

Because Seattle was only winning by six points at the time, the 49ers would have been able to kick an extra point for the game if the play had been completed. Richard literally changed the outcome of the Seahawks season on that one play. The play would also later be voted on by fans as the most significant play in Seattle Seahawks history, nicknamed "the Immaculate Deflection".

Seattle's victory meant that they earned a shot at the highly praised Denver Broncos. The Broncos were led by Peyton Manning and had one of the best offensive seasons in NFL history, heading into the Super Bowl. The match-up represented a meeting of the league's best offense against the league's best defense. Richard and his teammates spoke about how they were up for the challenge in the days leading up to the game.

In typical Richard Sherman fashion, he backed up his talk on game day. Seattle's defense had an impressive showing, shutting down the Denver Broncos offense throughout the entire game - only allowing eight points. In one of the most lopsided Super Bowl games in National Football League history, the Seahawks finished the game with a 43-8 victory. Furthermore, it marked the first Super Bowl win in Seattle Seahawks franchise history.

Richard was assigned to cover the Broncos' top receiver, Eric Decker, and held him to only a single catch. Richard also posted three tackles and showed great leadership on the field, despite it being his first Super Bowl appearance. For the entire postseason, Richard was only targeted six different times in a total of three games - a sign that opposing quarterbacks did not want to risk throwing the ball around him.

Following Richard's 2013-14 season, he was awarded the "Best Breakthrough Athlete" at the annual ESPY Awards. In the early off-season after his third professional campaign, Richard and the Seahawks agreed to a $57 million contract that would span four years. At the time of the signing, the contract was the biggest ever for an NFL cornerback.

Chapter 4:

Personal Adult Life

Richard is one of the most polarizing and unique players in the entire National Football League. His ability to trash talk with the best of them combined with the fact that he always backs up his talk, makes Richard a guy that opposing fans love to hate. However, once you understand what makes Richard tick off the field, it is truly hard to dislike him.

Richard really enjoys having fun off the field when he is not concentrating on improving his game. In a segment for Bleacher Report, Richard pretended to be an inquisitive journalist interviewing fans about who the better cornerback was, between he and Darrelle Revis. It was certainly humorous to see the responses that fans gave, especially the ones that were unaware that Richard was the one asking the question. This type of light-hearted behavior is what makes Richard so relatable to fans.

Richard is also a self-proclaimed nerd and has made it known that he enjoys reading and other cerebral activities. He has stated that he loves science fiction, particularly the Transformers franchise and the Halo video game franchise. Because of this, he was invited to attend the launch of the video game, Halo 4. He later found himself on the face of a video game, Madden 15, as the cover athlete for the season. Because Richard is so good at his position, he is actually one of only three players in the video game to have a perfect rating of 99, along with J.J. Watt and Calvin Johnson.

Chapter 5:

Philanthropic/Charitable Acts

Despite the fact that Richard has only been a professional athlete for a few years, he has already given back tremendously to many different communities. Amongst the charitable acts that Richard has engaged in, includes creating his own foundation. Richard has created the "Blanket Coverage Family Foundation". The goal of the foundation is to channel the funds that it receives into making sure that children who come from low-income households are able to receive an adequate amount of clothing and school supplies.

In order to raise funds for his foundation, Richard decided to create an annual celebrity softball game that he would host. He has been able to draw such big name celebrities as Kobe Bryant of the Los Angeles Lakers, Nate Robinson of the Denver Nuggets, and famous rapper Macklemore. The entirety of the effort includes a dinner in Seattle, followed by the charity softball game played the next afternoon. Along with the Blanket Coverage Family Foundation, funds received from this weekend also go to a few other charitable organizations.

Since the creation of his foundation, Richard has already helped nine different community centers and four schools. His goal is not so much charity as it is to level the playing field for these youngsters. Most other children take these essentials for granted and Richard wants to help give a chance at success to kids who would otherwise not have it.

However, Richard doesn't just give stuff to these children - he takes it a step further. He makes sure that the children sign a contract agreeing to improve their grades, stay attentive in class, not let their behavior drop, and keep their attendance up. In return, they will continue to receive the assistance. This accountability and incentive based philanthropic behavior seems to be the wave of the future, and takes charitable giving to the next step.

Richard has also visited the Rescue Mission in Tacoma, Washington. He spearheaded a large-scale donation of socks, shoes, blankets, books, and games to a total of 160 families. The families who benefited were suffering through homelessness and/or rough financial situations at the time.

Before even creating the Blanket Coverage Family Foundation, Richard had already developed the reputation as a guy who gives back without expecting anything in return. One example of this was when Richard saw a homeless man living under a bridge near the Seahawks' practice facility. Richard proceeded to go buy the man a meal at a nearby McDonald's.

Richard also returned to Dominguez High School to speak to the youth about the importance of education, staying out of trouble, and following your dreams. His impact was greatly felt in the community and many of the youngsters even talked about how they felt Richard changed the course of their lives through his talk.

Before creating his own foundation, Richard organized an event for the "Help A Hero Foundation". The event was held to raise funds in hopes to purchase a home for an injured soldier. A total of 7,500 people attended the event and it was successful in meeting its original goal.

Chapter 6:

Legacy, Potential & Inspiration

Despite that fact that Richard is still young in his professional career, he has already made a powerful impact in the stops along his journey. Since entering the National Football League, Richard has more defended passes and interceptions than any other player. Despite the fact that he is much less targeted now than he was early on in his career, Richard is still able to produce incredible statistics.

However, Richard has reached the elite level of playing defensive back in the NFL. This is shown by how his peers respond to his presence on the field. He is so good at covering his man that even quarterbacks like Aaron Rodgers and Peyton Manning try to avoid throwing the ball in his direction. The problem with this is that the other players in Seattle's defensive backfield, most notably Earl Thomas and Brandon Browner, are far from slouches. This forces quarterbacks into a tough predicament - either throw Richard's way or continue to test other elite defensive backs. This is not what kids dream of when they think of playing quarterback in the NFL.

While there is no doubt that his big hands, long strides, and impressive build allow him to cover opposing wide receivers, Richard earns his money because of his preparation and understanding of the game. Richard is an avid tape-watcher, focusing intensely on what the opposing quarterback and receivers tend to do. He keeps notes on every single NFL receiver and even has admitted to watching film in his bed. This superior attention to detail is what separates Richard from being just another decent corner and puts him in the discussion amongst the best defensive players in the entire game. Furthermore, Richard realizes that if he wants to set his legacy as one of the best cornerbacks to ever play the game, it will be his preparation and work ethic that get him there.

One of the ways Richard likes to out-smart opponents is by baiting the opposing quarterback. He knows how to intentionally leave a space between he and a receiver and act as if he is unaware that the player is open. In a quick series of events, Richard will get the quarterback to believe he has missed his assignment and then jump on his opportunity to beat the receiver to the ball.

While it is still hard to believe that Richard was the 154th pick in the draft, his ceiling appears to be very high. Because he has already accomplished so much in his young career and is playing for a top-notch organization, Richard can help make the "Legion of Boom" legendary.

As an aside, the fact that Richard is so intelligent and wears dreadlocks makes it difficult for prejudicial people to put him in a box, despite some that try so hard to. His eloquent speaking abilities and the fact that he is from Compton, Los Angeles, one of the most perceived "dangerous" places in the United States, show that we can not judge anybody based off of media-induced stereotypes. Richard is a role model in the utmost sense, only 26 years of age but wise and charitable well beyond his years.

Chapter 7:

Notable Statistics & Career Milestones

Here is a list of accomplishments that Richard has achieved in his young career so far:

- Super Bowl Champion (2014)

- NFC Champion (2014)

- Best Breakthrough Athlete ESPY Award (2014)

- Pro Bowl (2013)

- First-Team All-Pro (2012, 2013)

Conclusion

I hope this book was able to help you gain inspiration from the story of Richard Sherman, one of the best players currently playing in the National Football League. At the same time, he is one of the nicest guys outside the gridiron, willing to help out teammates and give back to fans. Last but not least, he's remarkable for remaining simple and firm with his principles in spite of his immense popularity.

The rise and fall of a star is often the cause for much wonder, but most stars have an expiration date. In football, once a star player reaches his mid- to late-thirties, it is often time to contemplate retirement. What will be left in people's minds about that fading star? In Richard's case, people will remember how he led his team in their journey towards a championship. He will be remembered as the guy who plucked his team from obscurity, helped them build their image, and honed his own image along the way.

Richard has also inspired so many people because he is the star who never failed to look back, who paid his dues forward by helping thousands of less-fortunate youth find their inner light through sports and education. And another thing that stands out in Richard's history is the fact that he never forgot where he came from. As soon as he had the capacity to give back, he poured what he had straight back to those who needed it, and he continues to do so to this day.

Hopefully you learned some great things about Richard in this book and are able to apply some of the lessons that you've learned to your own life! Good luck in your own journey!

Other Football Stories That Will Inspire You!

Calvin Johnson

http://www.amazon.com/dp/B00HJK0YS2

Tom Brady

http://www.amazon.com/dp/B00HJYQTRS

Aaron Rodgers

http://www.amazon.com/dp/B00HJUEDEI

Colin Kaepernick

http://www.amazon.com/dp/B00IRHHABU

Russell Wilson

http://www.amazon.com/dp/B00HK909C8

Peyton Manning

http://www.amazon.com/dp/B00HJUYTCY

Inspirational Basketball Stories!

Stephen Curry

http://www.amazon.com/dp/B00HH9QU1A

Derrick Rose

http://www.amazon.com/dp/B00HH1BE82

Blake Griffin

http://www.amazon.com/dp/B00INNVVIG

Carmelo Anthony

http://www.amazon.com/dp/B00HH9L3P8

Chris Paul

http://www.amazon.com/dp/B00HIZXMSW

Paul George

http://www.amazon.com/dp/B00IN3YIVI

Dirk Nowitzki

http://www.amazon.com/dp/B00HRVPD9I

Kevin Durant

http://www.amazon.com/dp/B00HIKDK34

Other Inspirational Stories!

Mike Trout

http://www.amazon.com/dp/B00HKKCNNU

Miguel Cabrera

http://www.amazon.com/dp/B00HKG3G1W

Buster Posey

http://www.amazon.com/dp/B00KP11V9S

Lou Gehrig

http://www.amazon.com/dp/B00KOZMONW

Babe Ruth

http://www.amazon.com/dp/B00IS2YB48

Floyd Mayweather

http://www.amazon.com/dp/B00HLEX5O6

Anderson Silva

http://www.amazon.com/dp/B00HLBOVVU

CPSIA information can be obtained
at www.ICGtesting.com
Printed in the USA
LVHW080350111220
673904LV00035B/730